Additional Praise for Tales of a Distance

"I am grappling with a road I once traveled," writes Andrew Gottlieb, and with keen perspective and honest reckoning he invites us to travel with him. Between parents and children, fish and fisher, hardscrabble origins and later comfort, here and there, rural and cosmopolitan, now and then. In his search for a moment's import, Gottlieb has the patience of a fly-fisher untangling a line to lay it back on the rod to be cast again and perhaps catch new meaning. The polished exoskeletons of these poems—beautiful and intricate in their workings—protect a vulnerable, self-aware soul as they sing. This book honors the work of a poet waiting to be sounded by—and sounding—the world.

—Elizabeth Bradfield, author of *Toward Antarctica* and *Once Removed*

Coyotes and winter vistas, plunging rivers and still lakes and the "salmon's black back"—Andrew C. Gottlieb has a keen eye and ear for the natural world, its vagaries and truths, but perhaps what's even more impressive about this poetic debut is Gottlieb's willingness to speak honestly about pain—his own, his father's, ours—and yet still try "[t]o find belonging / among the wet pebbles shifting in our palm [...]. / To try to name the question that memory / always is."

—Joe Wilkins, author of *Fall Back Down When I Die*, *Thieve*, and *When We Were Birds*

Andrew C. Gottlieb's Tales of Distance is an ongoing confrontation of the past with a sublime attention to the natural world. This stunning, poignant collection reveals the complicated relationship of father and son, the permeability of grief, and a desire for solitude— to follow the hawk, 'To find belonging / among the wet pebbles shifting in our palm'. Gottlieb's intimate, lyric poems are vivid and richly cadenced. In the liminal times of dusk, before sunrise, or at midnight, and with the speaker's gaze on the horizon reflecting on what slips away, here is 'the distance between trees and loss'.

—Suzanne Frischkorn, author of *Fixed Star* and *Girl on a Bridge*

Andrew C. Gottlieb frames his impressive debut with the long perspective, reminding us "lichen may thrive a thousand years." These poems recognize that the ways we live have consequences, and with a disarmingly beautiful musicality to his language, the poet stages domestic dramas against the backdrop of the more-than-human world of nature. Brutality exists here—"We already know each day brings / its glittering assault"—but the poet continually searches for provisional meaning, offering the possibility of hope for a place where we might plunge "safely into the ragged wildwood."
 —Todd Davis, author of *Coffin Honey* and *Native Species*

"Time is not light but layers," writes Andrew Gottlieb in the opening poem of this remarkable collection. And trace these layers we do, alongside him as he excavates his familial past and the plenty and violence of the natural world. He is a naked witness to fur and feathers, audience to the coyote's western anthem, watcher of soot and stars and trout and sawgrass. His poems find these layers in the names of things and in the whisper of romance in night's final landscape. This book is a wonder.
 —Jeffrey Thomson, author of *Half/Life: New and Selected Poems*
 and *fragile: a memoir*

Like Charles Wright, Andrew Gottlieb has a knack for taking the reader from the private restless turmoil of the internal world where "the clinging notes of home repeat" to the restorative mysteries of the external world where nature displays its "ever-changing slant of shadows/and what we imagine them to be." In this poignant and revelatory collection, the reader will travel a distance and back again through the anchors of the tangible and healing in the natural world to the griefs and hurt inherent in the history of a family and the inevitable ambiguities of the human soul.
 —Tina Schumann, author of *Praising the Paradox* and *Requiem* and
 A Patrimony of Fugues

Tales of a Distance

Tales of a Distance

poems

Andrew C. Gottlieb

trail to table press
eastsound, washington

Copyright © 2022 Andrew C. Gottlieb
All rights reserved

This book may not be reproduced or transmitted in any form by any means, electronic or mechanical, including photocopying and recording, or by any information storage and retrieval system. Excerpts may not be reproduced, except when expressly permitted in writing by the author. Requests for permission should be addressed to the author at andman1@hotmail.com.

First Edition. Published by Trail to Table Press
an imprint of Wandering Aengus Press

Poetry
ISBN: 978-0-578-35330-2
Printed in the United States of America.
Author Photo: Lisa Hu Chen
Cover Photo: Carl Gottlieb
Book Design: Jill McCabe Johnson

Trail to Table Press
PO Box 334 Eastsound, WA 98245
trailtotable.net
wanderingaenguspress.com

for Jenny

CONTENTS

I. PROLUSION: THE UNSEEN

Winter in Denali | 2

II. OPEN THROATS

Fugue for Wheelchair | 4
Perimeters | 5
Standing Patterns | 6
Sign Language | 7
Henry Moore's Seated Woman: Thin Neck, 1961 | 8
Amputations | 9
Close on the Range | 11
Portrait: The Seething of the Bedridden Man | 12
Open Throats | 13
Night Trees | 14
Coyote's Anthem | 15

III. FLOW VARIATIONS

Submerged | 17
On Mere Point | 18
The Gulf | 19
Landscape: North of Pavilion Key | 21
The Evening Meal | 22
The Walking Gods | 24
The Inner Wild | 25
Fellowship | 26
Blueprints | 27
Portrait: Parsing My Wife as Lookout Creek | 29
The Volcanologist Considers | 32
Ode to Smith Meadow | 34
March in Snoqualmie | 36

IV. TOURIST CANOE

Vagrants | 38
Tourist Canoe | 40
Orphans' Wake | 41
Halflives | 42
Naming the Everglades | 43
Late Winter: Metris for the Indistinct | 45
Evidence | 46
Room Service | 47
Delusion: As Equation for a Diminishing Vision | 48
Field Sermon | 51
Last Choice | 52
Leaving | 54
Cold Box of Night | 56
Ritual Leavings | 57
Metrics of the Long Night | 59
Superlatives, or a Brief Manifesto on Existence | 60
Finding Beauty, or a Science of Movement | 62

V. POSTCRIPT: OLD GROWTH

Tales of a Distance | 65

GRATITUDE | 66

ACKNOWLEDGMENTS | 68

ABOUT THE AUTHOR | 71

ABOUT THE PRESS | 72

> I don't know
> if it is age, or the simple knowledge
> that life is difficult, but it is not strange
> to me now that a man will excuse himself
> to go out into the little yard
> where he sits for an hour
> alone and mute trying to merge something
> in himself with nothing.
>
> —Charlie Smith, *Indistinguishable from the Darkness*

> We hid from the heat and talked of dying—the flickering boats our fathers rode to the spirit world, the little hulls of morphine.
>
> —Sandra Alcosser, *Except by Nature*

> In a way, every stranger must imagine
> The place where he finds himself—
>
> —Robert Pinsky, *An Explanation of America*

> There was even a time when he decided to go away and hide…He would first take a train, then after 200 miles get off and go about the villages. He asked an old pilgrim, a former soldier, how he traveled and how readily people gave alms and shelter…One night he even got dressed, intending to leave, but he did not know which was more right: to stay or to run away.
>
> —Leo Tolstoy, *Master and Man and Other Stories* trans. Paul Foote

I: *PROLUSION: THE UNSEEN*

Winter in Denali

Form is the woods…
            —Jim Harrison

Coats thicken, shaggy on caribou
and moose. Birch and aspen
shed theirs. Alaska holds still
its riches, the earth tightening its grip.
Storms spread stories, snow
softening the edges of everything,
hemming spruce and alder,
drifting into slope after slope.
The unseen curls warmly in sleep,
breathing slowly in secret dens.
The unseen leaves a ledger,
cuneiform grammar trailing
its language across snowed-over
taiga. The cold smells of patience.
What seems like little
is only a particular slowness.
Time is not light but layers.
Your hunger is not this hunger.
Dormant, then warm, then dormant,
a lichen may thrive a thousand years.

II: OPEN THROATS

Fugue for Wheelchair

We'd find my father sprawled on the hard wood
floor of the bedroom, fallen from his scooter—
as we called it, hoping names could make things
not what they were—and waiting for us
to return home grocery laden. I'm okay, he'd shout,
and heavy bags of food would drop. My mother's face.
Could she run. And he, amused at the refrain
of our concern as if the strains of panic
weren't the dissonance of fear and anger,
proof that leaving home could be a danger.
My parents wrestled with such tasks—balance lost
and found and lost—and me, I etched
the record's endless wound. The needle sticks
at times, the clinging notes of home repeat:
my father's careless laugh, my mother's pounding feet.

Perimeters

Life's locked in the ranch
    flat's paddock.

The west cliff's edge
    is its own fence.

Split-rail, stacked shack-side,
    rots, forgotten.

On the back porch one
    green chair

and a couple of snake-
    strung lights.

Who hasn't tested hinges
    with a gate-butting

thump? The trash can's
    stink brings

a slink of rodents
    in moon glare.

No one's ready for the mess
    of the morning,

the race of the day, eyes
    closed, head

lowered, another random
    gallop.

Standing Patterns

At the back porch, the screen door pleads
for grease to soothe the squeak. Hinges wait,
graceless, aching. In the invented West, tradition
dictates, a patience of things you never say

or do. A nuisance, roaches master cracks,
persistent as unmentioned failings. Her husband
hopes to ease the errant door ahead of supper.
Mother served fish fried straight, not fancy.

Each kitchen has its practice. She can strip a mess
of fish in minutes. Mother warned of men
who'll ask, they will. When guests assemble,
never speak of pests. She milks the slim fillets

the same way, egg, bread to hold the flesh.
Nighttime, she lies quiet while her husband mutters
feed store prices. The drawn hours weather
on. Quickly, she slips the fish in butter,

wary of the instant sizzle. At the bench,
he fingers grimy tools, bangs, rummages for oil.
These rules mother made: serve everyone
and wash the plates. *Mama, so much is*

false. Each mirror shows a season's rusting
rind. Old soap, a cloth. In the shower she wrings
her hair. The long day shifts, sucks in its breath.
She sees her limits milling at the fence.

Sign Language

She spoke to him with symbols
and bits of matter kicked
up, a shame because he was blind.
I'm a sell those horses.
His raised voice grated slivers
of her. Daytime, she waited
in the heat, sheets of summer
on her like blame. She watched
out the window the mares
again leave pasture.
His mutter: *Damn horse
can smell an open gate.*
Bacon fat set dull white
in a Mason jar by the stove,
and she knew in the evening
she would fry green-eyed potatoes
to black smoke and grease.
Often it was fast in the dark
and she would go soft
to avoid the hurt.
Her brittle hair in a knot
and her hands on her knees
at her chest. Each night
the herd limps back
on cracked hooves
to stamp regret in the dust
of the yard, and by morning,
like everything,
the chores remain.
Again, the bed hardens.

Henry Moore's Seated Woman: Thin Neck, 1961

Presenting: her neck stretching from turtle shell girth,
the pinched voice, quivering, trapped in the torso
that anchors her hips. She sways, tips,
legs blunted, stumps, struggling to shift her weight.
She bears protection. Assaults descend her arc
like water when she lurches from the tub,
cries tears on the couch on Sunday.
She has what she needs, and needs nothing,
and yet, from this shell, through this slim vent
she would slip if she could, escape,
trip away from the frame, and leave
the rock aslant. Her face twists.

Amputations

The widow clings, inverted, to her taut net.
Outside, the gray sky shuffles its displeasure,
a muddle of thunder clouds, the sulky sun
a sullen teen, a three-day runaway.
Cold oatmeal in a bowl and an empty
napkin holder. Her web stretches
to the baseboard corner. You wave your stumps,
scaring flies, a minor futility. What is life
now but lopped limbs, penitent greens wilting and limp?
All begging water. Her black abdomen shines
in the light, balancing elegance, arachnid tines
binding body to prey. Later, she'll eat
her mate. Picture your ambition of years
past. Now, in the meat of the night, your feet
make a patter amid photos, your family tree,
the crippled history you maneuver. A sting
in the air and a pang in your hip. In bed,
you flex the compass of your body, legs
spread, as if you spun sticky matter,
a safety net you could knit and grip.
The web is her nest; the air is her platter.
You could crush her with a hammer,
a gloved thump, a definitive swing
dictating limits. A tiny but total destruction.
Instead, you listen to the wind, squinting,
sensing the drying roots of a grimy youth.
The widow: she seems to float. You used
to count on straps, buckles, buttons, clasps.
Now, night sweats. Any kind of prescription.
What's her plan but a mingling of dominions?

The threat of mistaken identity, a clumsy
communion. A grip of teeth, an injection of magic,
a tragic step. Old milk and cold fish,
a dish of shredded cheddar. Her legs, her web,
the small red flag. Her wait is like yours,
an instinctual patience. Her view: the lines
on a circular map. What house is not also a trap?

Close on the Range

Coyotes ghost old pasture, the flats back of the slough.
Hazy roaming, their dusky way of taking,
brazen, able to dog through densest rot or hedge.
Guns clutter the basement. The acreage

sheds its fences. Used to be what moved got shot.
From the easy chair, legless father aims eyes
at family visits. Then quiet, this circling of signs:
empty glasses, a scavenger's tracks,

a crow complaining from the oak, missing a mate,
the granary, an easy meal. Persistent moon.
Mourning lost voices, buried days, last year's
grassy tasks. The ranch is vast, imagined.

He'll never see it all again. Blades rusting, long stuck.
The howls come late, testing the depth of the waning,
a bullet's range, messy plains unwalked,
the limits of a diminishing frontier.

Portrait: The Seething of the Bedridden Man

Another dim night at the periphery, in like a criminal—
quiet, transient—or the hitchhiker I'd rather be,
thumb up, stubborn, waiting, never in one place
for more than a piece of the day.
                                        I'd leave you, too,
all of you, shedding everything I had: berating pains
and numbness. Negate it. Erased, the way the night bullies
the day, smothering color at the window's lip.
Better yet, fake plates on a plain car taken from a lot,
the hospital, say.
                    These legs, wedged in the envelope
of a bed, sandbags lining truck beds.
                                       I'm through
with values. Truth, beauty, justice. Even evil is behind me,
muffled, sullen, shoved in a duffel, locked in the trunk,
struggling.
            I'll drift with the night like the rumor
of a crime. Nothing will catch me. Acquittal is my wind.
To desert what my life has dredged up from the sludge.
No more farce in the dark,
                        another crust gone stale.
Believe me, I'll cleave the flesh of this equation as I escape.
Watch me split the night's march with the heft of an ax,
leaving a deep cleft
                in the bed of my leftovers
while I race from the last slice of light, the given minutes
shading me, timing my end with snapping fingers,
their tedious winks,
                  the awful, clacking laughter.

Open Throats

I can hear them, those crows—
a sunrise cluster punctuating
the old black oak.

Like the coyote last night:
a hummock-strung howl—low,
solitary—that comes only when dark
has disguised the sloping shoulders
of the foothills.

What urges me out there?
Emigrant hermit: naked
witness to fur
and feathers at the hem
of the half-day, to open throats
preaching place
and a brazen intention.

The red-tailed rips the rabbit
pinned with slow black talons.
Clots of wet fur roll down
the dusty runlet.

There is this violence
in every light, these voices
at the window
crying, *see what I've done,*
crying, *run.*

Night Trees

The trees are there. The trees true me.
    —C.D. Wright

One frog, trilling his simple speech from the neighbor's place
while my wife fights sleep, afraid to miss
any kind of indictment or monotony. I do my best
to clasp the hand of night, a companionship,
blood brother to mile markers
and the ever-changing slant of shadows
and what we imagine them to be. Snakes in the road
and more often bodies, whole people, profiles,
faces, noses, shaggy wings spread in supervision
of my wife's dreams, most likely. She can dream up
emergencies like nobody's business,
and when her book hits the floor, there's relief
for everyone. It's then I consider walking barefoot
through the grass, under the night trees, sycamore,
fir, eucalyptus, any species of pine,
avoiding any man-made light, one more glance
at Venus, Jupiter, an ear for leaf scuffle, for any song
of the clan until my wife wakes in a panic.
What's happening? she'll demand, what's happening?
unaware of the stillness of a cedar,
the easy way I brush litter from the soles of my feet.

Coyote's Anthem

Out there, those hobo dogs squeal well before midnight;
whatever sets one off—his call cues the rest,
keening their homeless moans,
solo hymns strung
slope

to slope,
an orphans' chorus, mutts
touching the dark, vagrant notes
preaching or mourning above the musky desert,
songs like a migrant wind: roaming, flighty, blind.

III: *FLOW VARIATIONS*

SUBMERGED

Below the broad dock, beneath
    the scarf of mist,
the heavy cat settles
    in the black water.

It's the quiet like this I crave,
    before the sun
stabs at everything with its
    audacious knowing.

Early mornings, my father
    sat alone,
but could not teach
    what this meant.

The thick fish offers the slightest
    tailfin ripple.
Long whiskers wander the close
    pond bottom.

What choice for small eyes
    in the dark?
To try to read the muddy, unprinted
    ribbon of night.

We already know each day brings
    its glittering assault.

On Mere Point

Casting off the dock for stripers
I think of my father's stories—
fishing for walleye at Sioux Lookout.
The day a snapper ate his catch,
strung and struggling below the pier.
My hands feel for the telltale take
and I have to laugh. How two men
tooled of the same line
can argue themselves to silence,
watch reels unravel in a flickering tangle.
My fly rides from one moon phase
to the other side of the tide.
These baits are frail hope
that one dark mouth will take the hook,
end up caught in a cold bucket
of lost talk. Gravity sinks barbs below
the surface. As if the whole journey
was about the tug of men
and teeth to the trophy end,
as if—standing on this Maine
spit—it was only about one strung word
we could simply put our fingers to
and win with the slightest crimp
of a hissing drag. As if we don't swim
the same current: rod-stiff—muscles
tense and failing—until that glossy pose,
the wide stilled eye.

The Gulf

We are speaking of people, the charter boat captain
whose health is bad, the sweating nephew selling lychee roadside,
the slim, single math teacher with a limp, fifth-generation
descendent from homesteaders on the shell mounds.
Also, the fraction of dawn clutched between acceptance
and resistance, the way dusk, too, can feel like yours
or like a relative in Cuba, a rumor of history, as you watch
the evening light thin to a thing like latitude.

We are speaking of the difference between feeling and seeing,
feeling inside, but also the seven year-old boy who runs
in the sunlight, wants to touch everything,
his father annoyed, neck bitten again by the mosquito hunger
of the weighted shade along the two-track path,
a man who's long forgotten the joy of practicing
with a chisel, shaving skin-thin ribbons from a plank,
mastering the dove-tail joint, now bearing scarred fingers
and the stony profile of something carved,
a coral-like fossil in the bedrock of his forever-former self.

We are speaking of paying for it, moments quotidian
but quintessential, the way you sense the aged cashier
in the diner dockside has written you off
before you open your mouth to offer a sound,
a greeting or a pleading, the hinge we feel stiff
or swinging, the decision between hermit
and personality, whether to pull grief from its dry sack
below the hatch lid on the flats skiff.

We are speaking of when the son goes for the 'gator tail,
the way the father surges inside, considering a swing
at the idiot. The face at the window of the doublewide.
The potential objection of the chain-link gate
rusting next to a Beware-of sign. The way the horizon
can seem graspable or like wire strung with blurry barbs
of shadow, distant fists of pine lining limits

as the kitchen slants itself dark. The way the slow, gray horse
grazing evening weeds aside the plantation's dusty sedan
might once have known the shiver of choice
across its back, while down at the dock, an airboat
guns its engine, nosing toward the new angle
of evening, sucking up the last of the day
into hungry blades, shoving itself
to the thickening edge of an unasked question,
the stiff chin of night's ineluctable flood tide.

Landscape: North of Pavilion Key

When the wind dies over the low tide, it's a hot desert
on the slack flats.
The sea trout hold below in the turtle grass,
but the day's only bite is the slap of the sun's reprimand
coming off the water, singeing your face steady red
under a limp-brimmed hat for being out here alone,
for slipping the skiff
through the keys' curves
along the indistinct boundaries of distance,
angle to plane, red mangrove span to sand's gentle slope,
to land out on no land, the tender skin
of such glittering difference.
The silhouette of an unnamed bird floating
far starboard could be called reason,
but so can the taut voices
that surprise from behind
as you gaze to the gulf's horizon
where nothing can be seen,
nothing's there to anchor what you hear
in the sleepy heat
while you try to divine words: tern or shearwater
or fishing. Beneath, sand bars
lazily wait for their next invisible shift,
and as the late blue blaze begins to relinquish its best effort,
you squint to decide between island or eye-trick,
afterimage or schooling newness, about the bleary black shapes
speckling the southernmost edge of your perception.

The Evening Meal

The ceiling fan spins its whisper
in the day's decline. The lit lamp, a drink,
the curtains drawn across the glass.

You'd walked the water, casting line,
brushing away deer flies.

Such simple script, this thrown fly, the cast,
not left to right but to wherever you like
though always from here to there,
from dry hand to watery mouth,

the way you fed your father, hesitating at first
then comfortable, tipping up a spoon,
easing out a fork, maneuvering
these strange tools of union.

The feral mystery: what lurks under
the willow's limp limb? Cryptic,
the other. No question, you respect it.
Then nature in hand, the wild muscle,
the fish, thick as an arm,
wide iris, shiny sides scaled
with the faintest of lines, parr marks,
the maw of a mouth, dorsal spines,
tiny nostrils, fins magnificent and slick.

Of course, he never wanted to be fed,
and you never wanted to feed him,
and you both sat there knowing it,
but you had to agree
to a closeness you'd never been taught.
You both had to eat,
and perhaps you were more similar
than you'd ever considered.

So you tricked it, but it's already gone,
released with an easy slip to the ongoing flow.
You regret what's not still in hand,
the connection to the wild,
briefly revealed, then lost
for you can't keep any of it
if you want it alive,

and if he were, you'd feed him again
with a spoon, with the patience of a dim room,
the unwritten gift of a distant willow,
the weight of the day
a ghost on the plate of your palm.

The Walking Gods

The weight of the descending flow—cold, heavy,
dedicated to places downstream—confronts you
while you stare alone for giant cutthroat,
mythic, in the deepest pools.

There are gods in these woods, walking slopes
and meadows, the weight of seasoned legs
plunging spongy hole to hole.

A river never forgives, never compromises
its vision. The biggest boulders thunder
as they trundle on the bottom.

Deep in the old growth, there's a presence,
a recent breath, the deepest scent on rocks
left traced by the navigation of mosses.

The river's intimate tug presses
its indifferent love like a rope.
A walking stick and a steady step prevent
a drowning. Elsewhere, the tall gods
bustle. One stubborn bole leans over
like the oldest, strictest teacher.

The Inner Wild

Far away, I think of Wu Mountain Light,
blossoms ablaze and a clear warm river.
    —Li Po, trans. Hinton

Remembering alder along the river,
the shiver of aspen. Hiking the gravel
in the inch of water on the inside curve
of the river's whims. You were about to cast
and the moose stepped free from the tangle
of the far shoulder's willow.
      Later, the hawk
heading for the red cliffs, the whitetails
flushed as you crunch through the dry meadow.
The desire to follow. To find belonging
among the wet pebbles shifting in our palm,
the red spots on a brown trout's side.
To bed down in wild grass, to sleep with a river.
To try to name the question that memory
always is,
   black eye flashing in the mirror
that we are: untethered, flowing, gone.

Fellowship

Your friend says, God, I love women, and who's to argue,
the truck bouncing up the ruts and dips
of the two-track forest path on the bumpy plunge
to the river. The mysterious way we worship
what's missing, evening dreams considering angles
of flow, cut-banks, cryptic pools of dark, holy promise,
meander scars and the driftwood mark
of a periodic flood.
                       At the edge, we split, stepping
into the shallow lap—symptom of the serious current's
further water commanding the deep channel,
force that takes breath and balance with her only nature—
ready to clamber bankside over
                                   wet boulders, low limbs,
to reach the best eddies, but alone, we'll do it alone,
steady strive for the best heavy cutt in that volume
of cold motion,
            line tight to the wild other,
quest that brings us together only momentarily to relish
what we hope to briefly hold, blessing for which we sacrifice
one another: the sudden silver flash of bare muscle,
thrashing length in the day's hallowed splash.

Blueprints

Water, tools, and a new place,
swamp of sawgrass and talon,
long jaws and heavy reptiles.
I stand at the glass
and miss my wife.

It's not like walking on stage, mid-speech,
in medias res, and all that:
the spider's messy scene,
the toothy gape of a gator's monologue.

So much in this world will sting
if you push it. My wife
gets easily as tired of me as I of her,
and yet we'll both take each other's nest
over another feathered lair.

Soon, the mahogany hammock
may offer its metaphor.

Far away, my wife is surely working,
waiting for another day,
missing me, as I am her.

The plan calls again for words down
like wooden slats in a path
over the slough.

Spotted garfish hover
in the stained swamp water,
waiting for motivation,
a reason to lunge.

A new place is prologue, preface,
hunger. There is work to be done
to remove the newness
like sanding planks,
like intimacy.

Portrait: Parsing My Wife as Lookout Creek

My wife sits, wipes, stands, zips, forgets to flush.
                                                          Rushing,
the river's every agenda. We pull at our clothing,
    all day, humans, us,
                all of us.
                        Try not to touch it.

I stand at the mirror, tuck a tail, a tag, tug a collar, flinch.
    What face is that?
                  Dry
outside, there are pines pushing against every reflecting sky
    in their own grim time.

My mother, tough one, British stiff.   *Sit up straight. Excuse
    you. That's a dessert spoon.*
                              Butler's fool,
ambassador for a childhood of rules.   One tough one.

Language gets us in its grip with its little links and latches,
    clasps, clamps,
                padlocks,
                      and we're lost: grappling.

Close your mouth when you chew.
                            In these river days,
what floats for me to find is the tissue, wet, a red filmy swirl
    the symptom of a drifting of cells
                          alluvial shift
in a body I know.

                    Do you imagine first the conifer leaves?
Or the buried thread-like roots
    deeply reaching for food?
                        Plunging to touch the hidden skin
of the river.
            Dawn's lazy diffusion of hues lights the children's
confusion, their breakfast food,
            flow
                        of this river that spews
stripped trunks, a shoe, crescent crust of dead everything,
the ongoing plunge of innards and corpse.

Even my stepdaughter laughs, who for now laughs last,
                                        least.
There's nothing funny about PMS: period.
                        My wife,
sure, she blushes, but it's love like the cat's torn mouse,
    the breast-split wren,
                the rejected owl pellet,
                            her kind of love,

the river's necessary way of sharing of what she's composed,
    unburdened by grammar, maps, latitudes, rules,
banks.
        I am wading
                the lava rock and free-stone bed,

the old-growth bole
            wedged
                        and lecturing only by collecting
every drifting thing that the muscle spits up, aggregate of flow,
    motion of bundling,

clustered abundance of the rushing's best refuse.

                                                    I steady my step,

pocket a bottle, sift the river with my fingers, sink
   into its stunning flood,

                        touch her every part.

The Volcanologist Considers

Far away, the elk are little spots of beige light
    shifting at the base of the ridge
as if on some strange ice, the way we skate
    our own lit dimensions, one foot out,
a glance behind, a guess at the right next step,
    a question for the tribe
that's around us and nowhere all at once
    as the sun's face comes clean
from behind the cloudy mask, plane of light
    doubling the ridge's limb
with sudden shadow. Some of us make decisions
    while others wait for an instigator,
trusting to fate, neither of which is a guaranteed
    strategy for success.
The flycatcher sitting in the alder dives and eats
    before we've even seen the insect,
but there are times we wish deer didn't think so much
    about headlights, spot lit and calm
as something unknown in the near dark rumbles
    from an indistinct location,
stretching its chest, testing the night's boundaries,
    indifferent to the potential
for death or collisions of a messy organic nature.
    Trout rise, little fists of black
as the hatch lifts off the pond water, feasting
    on emergers, midges, motes
of light, and perhaps disturbing the surface
    at a cellular level for an instant
before molecules pull themselves together
    again. Sometimes my wife's

protestations feel seismic, intended to challenge
    my very nature, my disposition,
when what she means is, I miss you, but the language
    takes a different tack, bullying
its way through a simple evening at the kitchen sink
    as the last sunlight angles itself
from the scene. If we're wise, we may realize how thin
    is our own meniscus, sensitive
limit between us and other, the line between attack
    and retreat where we determine
how to endure the fragile space with patience,
    or perhaps knowing the best
decision is to walk away from the favorite place
    at the base of the volcano.

Ode to Smith Meadow

I miss Fish Creek,
meadow stream
waist-thin, bent
again under shaggy
banks, slanting grass,
hanging weed
and alpine flower,
swale-placed stream
with a headwater
chill, chiseled
pasture channel
canyon-bound, down-
ward tending, slope
only slight at Sierra
heights, angling
as gravity asks,
pooled in places
sheltering trout,
showy goldens,
fingerlings, larger
fish, elders that winter
over, lingering,
invisible, then leaving
rings, rippled
dimples, sipping
surface bugs under,
midges, nymphs
close to the wing,
hatches of rapid
miniatures filling

the low sky, cattle-
high, drifting pollen-
like over the scene,
Fish Creek, Smith
Meadow, acrobatic
swallows, the herd,
slumbering,
what sways in me
in that place, all
of us grazing
the gift of the
recumbent day.

March in Snoqualmie

Just before the Middle Fork, four elk trot
    across the single-path gravel,
unmapped road, winter's shruggy humps
    and shaggy coats in passing,

ample shudder, last antler, muscled neck
    of the cold's steamy nose,
memory of snow, before the overflowing
    banks of the swelling spring.

IV: *TOURIST CANOE*

Vagrants

Those coyotes—
silent
tonight—
usually bold

gossips, probably
acres
away,
long gone

after rabbit—
the sprint,
panting—
or other scent

on mustard stalks,
ragged
chaparral,
the desert's palm.

Only crickets,
a rat's
scrabble,
the faintest wind.

Midnight's empty den
cradles
my patience;
what day's end

without the howl?
Brazen
claims,
a desperate prowl,

dog-declarations
of love,
hunger,
rutting, straying;

a fragrant trail,
soft
paws,
exhalations

after the hunt:
bloody,
other-
wise. Vagrants,

all of us, restless
in drought
for sound
of animal fuss

and wrestle. Groggy,
bleary-
eyed, ears
pricked, mock dog.

Tourist Canoe

Always like this: the thunk of paddle on gunwale.
Angled wood turns pond drip to ripples,
and the curved bow spears the surface
in a silent glide ahead of the pressed blade.
This is you alone, your body levering the boat,
hull rolling with tensed intention,
hips shifting with the lean and lull of the shell
on clear water, the slow growth of the far-off shore.
In the bow, a bag of rock for balance. The surface
resists your sink with its broad flare, your float:
this delicate measure of spread and pressure.
Below your stroke, boulders sit in green depth,
glacial remains dragged and dropped
with an age that makes you afraid. This is you,
alone, skimming the surface again
with what flexed effort your body allows mere feet
from the cold underneath the lake reveals.
A pause to consider the dark fish floating
over the rock you fear, the salmon's black back
still for a moment in the slack lake, the long body
almost invisible, hovering mid-water
below your boat before a gill-flare and a rippling fin
tip you off to the flicker of a swift single surge.
You stare: there's just a rock, and this is you, land-locked,
adrift with your lean and your look, your shadow,
the paddle, your stiff imitation.

Orphans' Wake

Orphaned again, each evening
we circle the burning
on the beach,
eager to ring the fire,
turning out clouds and rain,
the long face of an early winter.
Around us, the sky flings
its arrogant weather
like a dress,
hiding the horizon's
low islands with its hem.
The same way
we ostracize our losses
by turning our backs
and knotting our fingers
around a dance of spark
and flame, our altar of light
and loss. We throw our bones
to the coals. We clutch
at combustion and wait all night
for the grey remains.
We carry them home, carry it
forever: the weather,
the ring, the light, the damp ashes
we bring with us everywhere,
carrying them in our mouths
for the sooty taste
of every thing that burns
and stays.

Halflives

Perhaps it's the dust at the cuffs of the walls.
I'm neat but I'm not clean.
                              Clans.
Family farther and farther. Cabinets
stacked with cans no one moves.
                                      Dishes
collect on the counter like debt.
                                  Overhead, the bed
bangs, some small boat riding the surf
into pilings.
                No doubt the water stain
on the ceiling tiles is spreading.
                                  Coffee grounds
and sour milk and orange peels.
                                  Laundry piles.
Rooms, a rot of molecules. At the sink,
sleeves slip down my arms
like a shudder,
                drown in the slate lake.
I feel for the knives that hide by the drain.

Naming the Everglades

I could talk about the biology, the taxonomy,
the scientific names of things—
delicate biodiversity of Latinate costume—
but all I really know is the acres and acres of sedge
stretching away to the eyes' horizon,
so much of it untouchable,
the plains that make these glades,
and the way I'd like to walk out among them,
stepping wetly wild, brushing the side
of one distant, vase-like cypress: leaning greenery
of grey slightness. So much of the world
holds itself at a distance, the woman
with binoculars walking alone off the path,
the teacher who never made eye contact,
the quiet chat you had before your grandfather
disappeared into an Iowan sky,
the moon, the stars,   *(what are they?)*
and perhaps we need Latin names
to aid us, Linnaeus with his intricate system,
labels that may assist with listing, specificities,
but not with wandering hungrily in the mud
of things, the urge to slather it over skin,
to grab at other people and hold them to our body
with an unfashionable grasping
that doesn't ease in any way the sense
with which we're left, a recurring awareness
of insignificance when confronted
by a vast landscape of hammock and sawgrass.
Or by a call, the hidden hawk, red-shouldered
and solitary, offering an uncategorized cryptography

we can only translate as awe, richness,
epiphany about so many boundaries,
none of which will ever be grammatical
or constellate, but always slipping invisibly away
to the drifting grass that seems just inches
from your fingers, the humbling limits
of your outstretched, hoping hand.

Late Winter: Metrics for the Indistinct

Broad swath of early frost across the kitchen panes,
glass coated with cold, night's final landscape
treeless but textured,
frigid mimetic for the winter ridge
distant in the dim morning.

The old man genuflects bedside
in gray light, questions
like prints trailing off in old snow.

Above the spruce, sun, not yet over the ridge,
shows itself not as itself
but as a sign of itself
in the pink flush of the clouds
that gather and shift, uneasy.

The young girl, back-flat in taiga snow,
flings arms into wings,
then flips over, makes moose hooves
of her mittens, crawls across the soft cold,
says, *Watch me stomp*,
then pauses, looks to the black spruce
as if something's suddenly appeared,
is standing there, watching us,
wondering what, exactly, we are.

EVIDENCE

Let's finger dreams, maybe in the way of gift shops,
souvenirs, as if somehow, after the tour, pause here,
an object-option of the magic places that clutch us
in the night. Scary, otherwise, so much of the drama
is rain, slanted in the late day, scurrying its way
to attributes like damp that speak to past
staggerings, symptoms of something, the way wind
tells us of invisibility. What I'd like is objects
showing up in the house, suspicious things:
car keys with a worn nylon fob, a can of cat food,
its label in Arabic, lavender underthings
draped over the fish tank, a leather folder
of photos, fading. So much goes unremembered
in this creative making-up of lives, the brain
story-boarding its way through the stigma
of night. The next time my wife says, Dreams,
want to know? I'd like to point and say, Look.
Half a baguette from Paris, someone's suede shoes,
a knife, shiny, from that shadow that was chasing me,
and maybe in the backyard, a llama on a rope,
grazing the wet grass, and we can say not just, Hey,
it rained, but Hey, it rained while you farmed alfalfa
in Argentina, married a Persian queen or king, then leapt
off that cliff, escaping fatefully from the grim shade
that drifted so quickly, the menace that returns,
leaving their dark robe in the laundry basket,
their myth and mysterious longing, dirty, in the sink.

Room Service

Always: beds in hotel rooms like deaf wives, late arrivals,
overpriced red wines from room service, old pillows
and a clock that's off.
                      You've forgotten which airport
you're in, a pleasant stasis you embrace
like a mild narcotic. You follow cartooned arrows,
the cabriole calves of a woman with purpose,
the faint yearning
                for the awning of an angular body.
It's not a love novel. It's exhaustion and a carry-on,
the anonymous seething of people unwilling to touch.

The spine of your life with its mollescent lessening,
the sycamore leaves in an October street
                        like an old man's
hands.
     Your plea: turn from these things, turn
it back into a romance. That's the version you want,
the magic of mistaken identity, collapse at the bar,
the traipse to a trim room and long view of the dark bay,
the small white lights,
                a fallen constellation. The menu
tells lies. Each glacial day slides to its end, taking
everything with it, these people,
                  your children.
You order cabernet, a sunrise, a forest of sugar pine,
the red-head you met two decades ago, and you'll sign
for it all, far away,
              in a small place of which you've heard,
some dreamy, temporary country.

DELUSION: AS EQUATION FOR A DIMINISHING VISION

One of the last great realizations is that life will not be what you dreamed.
        —James Salter

Pencil it: the equation might give you an inkling
of the vision you exist in, a picture
that's beyond your reluctant recognition, actually delusion,
another muddled movie eluding truth, your starring role
as a substitute, a B-rated supernumerary.
Your fed-up wife in bed, reading a novel, coughing.
Your life, a week of Wednesday nights, your children,
afraid of anything but lights on brightly in the cluttered
hallway.
        One day, a day ago, really, just yesterday, you were on stage
reciting lines from a play: *Sexual Perversity in Chicago*,
or any town, near you, coming soon, and they were just words.
You saw no reason to be afraid as the play indicates
you should. Time enough to play act someone else's life,
their fright, those imagined long nights, sparse writing,
a violent dialogue you understudy.
        Mistaken. Erase it: the variable
is years, solve for years, the x at the end of the equals. Symbols
and signs of the dull plot you plod in a pot
of hot milk, your spoon scraping the bottom, stirring to prevent
the slick skim from spreading, and always at the top,
a speck of black marring the smooth surface of 3 A.M.,
early Thursday again.
        Your routine: plastic trash cans
curbside. The car curving to work in that long leftward blur.
Later, you read as long as you can, descending away
from your spat with the daytime. Tussle done:

you're a fattening slut for the drug
of fatigue. You fight to mate with the night, the quiet.
                                        Your math
is bad, and in the dark of the yard, the shrubs are slowly growing
over the graves of dead pets. You're sure it was only one day—
one short day—ago you heard someone call, "Places,"
you heard the word, the stage manager's ministrations,
but this spotlit train is not stationary
but heading away from the station you dreamt
at a pace excruciatingly fast and slow, both,
a quantum quadratic toasting in the bar car your own slowness,
meaning: awareness it pains you to equate with ignorance,
however you couch it.
                    You're a sloth, long claws curled
at the cool trunk for security, sleep, not as an option,
but as collision with your unconscious, and you want it heavy,
deliberate, hours of your day drowned in delirious
concoction. Hot milk. You laugh, your grandfather's tonic.
There was a day you could drain a bottle of Scotch
at a table, telling tales, and wake for a jog.
                                        Now, the day
is a fog of exhaustion: forget the narcotics, you're a log, muddy
at the bottom of a stagnant pond. Waterlogged with poor health
and other insurance, a curse of paperwork, forms and formulas
for the value of your life.
                        That number: was not in the script.
You crave the vague rehearsal; your blunt children shun you.
Waver across the room, water the plants, catch the sunset
at seven. The day closes over the hatchings you've scratched.
It happens like that. The penciled directions,
                                    the curtain,
a certain decisiveness culled from the calculus you're working

while the stove heats, the milk steams, and you stir,
your heaving chest easing like a turned-off burner.
The burden you fear: a failure at forty
                              in the shade of
your ancestors' past: silver dollars, golf gloves, a farthing, a pfennig,
a black cane of pine wood. Leather books. It's all long gone
at the pawn shop. You never knew what to save,
and why would you? It was all just a play. You're left
awake at the end of the day with your blank face
and pencil shavings thin and wrinkled as dead skin
whittled from your busy fingers,
                          worn digits you wish were wings.

Field Sermon

You can ask the moon
for anything: shout, scream! Mice
will still build their nests.

Last Choice

Reading the long night again and feeling bare about it,
as if its dark secrets pare away as well at mine, clever knife
skinning the cape off these grand selves we nudge
down the runway. My wife snoring, rasping,
creating a soundtrack to her steady exhaustion;
every time she goes silent, I'm afraid she's died. I watch
for the lift of the blanket, take a sip of an IPA so strong
it smells like pot. I try to decide whether to write a line
or read another poem. Tonight, today, tomorrow:
the anniversary of my father's death, his life's last choice.
We stood in shock and watched, supporting his decision,
stunned to say hello when, at intervals, his eyes opened
from a morphine stupor. He knew he was back each time,
he hadn't forgotten the drifting off to deeper water.
Once he actually said, I'm glad to be back,
which broke my mother, and she agreed she was glad,
too, even though by then all bets were off; he was so drugged
that *back* was a momentary state just steps away
from a permanent unconsciousness. No one can teach me
more about life or death than my father did, though
his hands were mostly full; inadvertant lessons came my way.
My wife goes silent again and I check her, thrilled
to see the gentle arcs of the red blanket. Life: this woman
makes it somewhat bearable, I think, this one
who knows my secrets and hangs around, remembering
the days I've called from the dark side of a house,
unable to talk. We laugh and tell each other cute,
ridiculous things, terms of endearment, nicknames
that outside of us sound absurd. Once, on a slow afternoon,
I said someday maybe we should choose joint suicide,

that neither should grieve, that we could go together,
synchronized, a passive dance, a real date, with no fear
of commitment. I didn't elaborate, figuring it would scare her
and make me sound insane, but she nodded.
What she heard was, I will die for you, and honestly,
I know it can be done: my father did it for himself and for us.
People shrug off the option, fingering courage as the lack,
the flickering bulb of weakness. Courage is a lesser
sidekick to pain, though, and now I watch again my wife
breathe. Quickly death comes on its own schedule,
and some days it feels like so little keeps me from raving,
nakedly, giving up, stripping down and never returning
to the halls of composure. I cross my fingers, pay our bills,
dance with my wife. Eight years ago he died
and it's like yesterday. It's how you know you're alive,
when the memories stay, vivid as the stiffest of drinks.
Like yesterday, we say, when you're faced with a certain
last time, when your wife goes silent,
when you know all too well what that might mean.

Leaving

I packed a truck the year my father died
and, with my brother, drove for weeks. Our leaving
seemed a reasonable fact, a movement
for its own sake from the silence
that had visited the family as teacher
and taker.
                Every day we left new places,
packing our containers in a mundane trance
of ice in a cooler, food, and fuel.
One early morning in a Kentucky lot, we laughed
at nothing, and another car sped off, local folks
assured of our insults, showing us fingers
and angry faces, as if these two quiet drifters
wielded petty jests.
                We headed west
into wind and the sense of a fearsome freedom,
abandoned to weather and its battering,
fast-moving dust storms with ragged edges
and gritty cliff-high walls that defined
nothing but blindness and the taste of ashes.
Vagrancy isn't a narrative task.
                It's a trough of sand,
a hand in your face. We slept in rocky grottoes,
in the shade of sloping dunes that scalloped
the horizon and every fading light.
In Missouri, a mechanic fixed a flat
for forty dollars while we mapped town names
as if things mattered beyond sound,
the rhythmic patter of the pavement,
the clack of pebbles in deep wheel wells.

Leaving
was what really counted and the chanting
of the act. He asked to leave us;
he'd had pain enough. We had no atlas
for consent so we were left to ask, What place
is this? And he was gone. The house demanded
not a thing: we packed our bags.
                            In a Colorado corner
we hiked empty ruins, Anasazi hauntings,
mud-made cliff-side rooms that bade us sit.
Around us: forest fires, pot shards scattered
in the desert sand. The arid carved-out country
like a crumpled sheet.
                            We dug a water well by hand
a thousand feet, planted maize on mesa tops,
and floated over canyons, sending tribal howls
out to do our leaving, to echo far and long
and call the family home.

Cold Box of Night

The couple knows limits of the cold,
of each other,
of weather,
of the way the sun lifts only once
each day,
that the rest
may be a riding onward of the sled,
dogs lunging,
legs hungry,
crunching over the dry snow
to a still
and silent
horizon, a cold box of night,
dark
corners,
the dim cover of winter's thick book
beckoning
trespass,
old stories of fish in a pot,
the wind's
whispers,
words like *match*, words like *fire*.

Ritual Leavings

We went to your stone and waited.
    The snow showed our past,
        gave us away in our giving.

Block letters, bright sun, frozen grass.
    Winter was listening
        while we lined our things

along the short granite cliff.
    Three chocolates in lockstep,
        a latte, a small happy Buddha,

the three-dollar kind in red plastic
    with his bag and his look.
        A small book of poems.

The only things missing: new photos,
    your laughter. This losing
        dismantles our notions of wholeness,

cold fingers, a frivolous mingling,
    a single crow hunched in an oak.
        Who's not lonely in the cold?

The trees have retreated excepting the firs
    with their green skirts and thin leaves.
        Needles, the decline, goodbyes, pine

scent. You've left us behind
>to a ritual leaving. A comb,
>>a coin, an orchid, bone whistles.

A milling of beliefs at the coldest
>of stone, our clinging past
>>like a piling, a raft, and a rope.

Metrics of the Long Night

I can't tell anymore. Which is long and which is short,
the river flowing east or thoughts farewell brings on?
               —Li Po, trans. Hinton

Realizing your father's been gone seventeen years,
gray elision like early night's blind spot,
a last crow just winging back
to roost in the tidal marsh.
It catches your eye, the angle of a feather,
impression of movement in the corner
of the room. Asking nature what's real,
demanding metrics: counting cricket chirps,
scritchy wings sawing off bits of evening.
Measuring the sun at last setting
with a thick thumb as if touch
was possible. Remembering lightning
and the count to thunder: children's game
testing terror. How close the storm?
We feel the unknowns raising their hands
as if answers lingered just off the path,
as if the foothill's wind was a classroom.
A brief wing flap from the roof's hidden slant,
the dog's one bark from the house
on the hill. Along the ridgeline, a coyote
shuffles and whines, nose to the dirt,
moon-dog pawing for anything alive.
There is unnamed awakening
in every dark corner. With a bent head
in the long night, we listen carefully.
We hope our ghosts will show.

Superlatives, or a Brief Manifesto on Existence

People will tell you how things are the best this
or the best that, the best kimchi in San Diego,
the best ribeye in Cincinnati,
and even about other people: the best geologist in Beijing
or the best plastic surgeon ever—*trust me*;
while here, at the hot edge of the swamp,
the big event of the day is the afternoon rain,
and I head to the porch to watch the first slow, white streaks,
though the clouds have been piling, promising more,
and soon it really shows up, loud on the roof,
the ground, the dripping and tapping a deluge of sonal variety
like hundreds of tennis balls all dropped at once
amid thunder and new puddles; the air is blurred
with so much moving water that the day
turns grayer, takes a static texture, like bad reception
on an old TV. Occasionally I'm jealous
of those people who are continually discovering the best
of everything, the best ice cream, the best lawyer,
but I think they're in for a let down
when they realize it's a bit of a construct,
not to mention a simplified yardstick: things either the best
or they're not measuring up. Part of me wants to try
and say, *This* is the best rain ever,
since I'm not sure anyone's ever said that
except perhaps really thirsty hikers or scientists
taking specific measurements, but the truth
is that it's an enjoyable storm because I'm here to watch
with not much else to do. I sit in a chair
and consider the weather, much in the way I hope
to view future storms. It seems to me no matter

what occurs in the world there's someone doing it better
somewhere, and that probably goes for processes
as well. Frank sang "The Best is Yet to Come"
and the song is catchy, but I'm not even sure that's true,
though I admire optimism. Who's to say, really.
What seems worth doing in a given moment
is sitting on a porch watching a storm do its business.
Later an impressive humidity will fog my glasses
when I leave to find groceries, and overall it's fair to report
that another day in the Everglades has been simple
yet varied, untradeable for any steak in L.A.,
or buffet in Vegas, or TED talk via podcast,
and if—on the road tonight—I witness a possum's
yellow eyes in my headlights before it scuttles off
into the wet green wall of the swamp,
I'll be about the happiest man I think I can be,
give or take, you know, some of the being, the happy,
the general est-ness of our brief time
amid these ongoing, evolutionary matters.

Finding Beauty, or a Science of Movement

It's not just for the driving, but the yearning
to return to the long highway, two-lane
through ranch land rising into foothills,
the earth's thick, sloping limbs that survey
the entire quest; I'm not there
but want to be to see the antelope,
the tawny idea of catching the flexure
of legs, of approaching something so wild
that twice like it never exists,
but being the victim of it once makes you ache
with inner, repetitive begging,
the kind of thing that requires you to lie
all day to survive the pedestrian taunting
of email replies, the drive to work, accountability,
and always the questions of weather,
each small paving stone you place
only to try to counter imminent chaos—
you think of the earth's surface,
the declivities, faults, volcanoes,
insistent spew of variables in the glacial equation
of geologic change, the tectonic tonnage,
the gallons, the light years—while inside,
it's the road, the antelope, the moment
where there are long bare reaches of animal option
and promise. I am here, and always a road
is not a point but a going, a creature sort of like light,
a particle and a wave, immeasurable, really,
while it's happening, the journey only visible
from the symptoms on some end paper showing shadows
and patterns, suggestions of what mystery

actually occurred, what magic collided
and collapsed to later cause this pain.

The black-eyed herd reclining in fallow grassland,
soil yellowed by afternoon sun,
and there are two directions
where I am: the road lining off
to a far horizon, and from where I came,
the mythical place where I may believe it was all okay;
but I think, I could run this way, too,
I should step into this dust and run,
the way the herd does when I stop the car
because pronghorn know something about sound
and closeness, and they won't let it happen,
and I can't stop them, and everything is far away,
and I'll want it back, this sejant-erect
idea that guides my understanding, this human
failing that aches, and the drive to feel it
again and again, to have the moment last
rather than transfer itself to memory
and its yearning, the weakness that pulls me back
from the now to the herd, to their leaving: white stripes
hurdling cattle fences in easy leaps.
They take it with them, distance eclipsing
what I thought I had and what's already gone,
what's become a measurement and a guessing,
the road and the antelope, mammalian sorrow
fossilized no matter how we dress it or where we go.
Evolution. Call it love, call it loss, even hope.
It's slow resistance to motion and the sadness of nouns.
I am grappling with a road I once traveled
and, quite literally, the only physics I know.

V: POSTSCRIPT: OLD GROWTH

Tales of a Distance

Like a fear, or a love, the elk keep returning to him,
    tapping
hooves in a soft trot across the road,
    the roaming
road coursing his forests like a lateral line,
    a fishy
sixth sense he's only begun to learn to trust
    amid
the day's murky stain, the wind, the invisible current
    narrating
place, tales of a distance unstrung from rusty fencing,
    freed
from mud-thick cut bank that might suggest
    boundaries,
physical limits, the whys of his failure to grasp
    in his hand
the horizon, a mist, the distance between trees
    and loss
while waiting again for the steaming nose, the wet
    brown eye,
the thick, rough coat of the winter beast pausing
    at the odd road,
checking for any sensed threat, any testing soul,
    then loping
over again, plunging safely into the ragged wildwood
    of unmeasured depth.

GRATITUDE

I'm grateful to many people—artists, family, friends, teachers—who've helped shape these poems and/or offered support, inspiration, guidance, or friendship that's kept me going. It's too large a community to list all, but specific thanks to:

Jill McCabe Johnson, Tina Schumann, and everyone at Wandering Aengus Press/Trail to Table Books for bringing the manuscript to life.

The many editors who published the poems individually.

AIRIE (Artists in Residence in Everglades), Artist Trust, Beargrass Writer's Workshop, Denali National Park, the H.J. Andrews Experimental Forest, Isle Royale National Park, Kimmel Harding Nelson Center for the Arts, Montana Artists Refuge, Seattle Arts Commission, and The Spring Creek Project.

Iowa State University and the University of Washington.

Karen Leona Anderson, Christopher Arnold, Larry Benesh, Tom and Norma Benton, Linda Bierds, David Bosworth, Allen Braden, Elizabeth Bradfield, Heidi Brown, Kim Buehlman, Simmons Buntin and the Terrain.org family, Katherine Captain, Rob Carney, Kurt Caswell, Po Sun and Lisa Hu Chen and family, Erika Cherrier, Dr. Yujuan Choy, Jim Cokas, Charles D'Ambrosio, Todd, Noah, and Nathan Davis, Alison Hawthorne Deming, Cinnamon Dockham, Chris Dombrowski, José, Steve, and the Donovan family, Amy Fleury, Suzanne Frischkorn, Bharti Gupta, Charles Goodrich, Jim Harvill, Andrew, Brenda, Jon, Simon, and Chris Hawes, Rebecca Hoogs, Parkman Howe, Charles Johnson, Kathy Keable, Joan Labrosse, Joelle Labrosse Jordan, JP Labrosse and the late Gerard Labrosse, Debbie Lacy, J. Drew Lanham, Benson Lee, Radha Marcum, Deb Marquart, Heather McHugh, Kevin Miller, Pooja Minutaglio, René Mogensen, Ander Monson, Niren Murthy, Julie Nelson, Charlie Rathbone and family, Nick Rathbone and family, Pat Rathbone, Daniel J. Rice, Rick, Sally, and Anna Rivero, Peter Robison, Dick and Mary Scheibe, Doug Schnitzspahn, Derek Sheffield, David Shields, Andy Simmons, Cheryl Slean, Maya Sonenberg, Michael G. Smith, Lauren Springer, Heath Stoyle and family, Fred Swanson, Violeta Tauragiené, Michael G. Tasios, Jeffrey Thomson, Eric Usner, Keith D. Waddington, Hazel Walker, Matthew Wilemski, Nicole Wilkin, Joe Wilkins, and Ericka Wolf.

My mother, Margaret, and my late father, Carl. Warren and Julie Fan. Brother Steve and his family: Jill, Miles and Theo Gottlieb. Roger Fan and family. The extended Gottlieb and Buchan families far and wide.

Jenny, Sebastian, and Madison who've made my life far richer than I could have expected.

ACKNOWLEDGMENTS

Individual Publications

Apostrophe
    Henry Moore's Seated Woman: Thin Neck, 1961
Best New Poets 2013
    Portrait: Parsing My Wife as Lookout Creek
Briar Cliff Review
    Sign Language
    Submerged
Chautauqua
    Winter in Denali
    Cold Box of Night
Crab Creek Review
    On Mere Point
Day One
    Leaving
DIAGRAM
    Fugue for Wheelchair
    Halflives
    Orphans' Wake
Ecotone
    Tourist Canoe
The Flyfish Journal
    Ode to Smith Meadow
The Hopper, online
    Late Winter: Metrics for the Indistinct
ISLE
    Open Throats
Portland Press Herald
    On Mere Point
Mississippi Review
    The Gulf
The New Purlieu Review
    Delusion: As Equation for a Diminishing Vision
Poecology
    March in Snoqualmie
    Field Sermon

Poetry Northwest
    Evidence
    Naming the Everglades
    Night Trees
The Portland Review
    Standing Patterns
San Pedro River Review
    Room Service
Sierra Nevada Review
    Perimeters
Sugar House Review
    Ritual Leavings
    Coyote's Anthem
Talking River
    Close on the Range
    Tales of a Distance
Tampa Review
    Amputations
Verse Daily
    Halflives

ANTHOLOGY PUBLICATIONS

Awake in the World: A Collection of Stories, Essays, and Poems about Wildlife, Adventure, and the Environment
    Tourist Canoe
Campfire Stories: Tales from America's Nat'l Parks, Vol. 2
    Naming the Everglades
Cascadia: A Field Guide through Art, Ecology, and Poetry
    The Walking Gods
DIAGRAM II
    Halflives
DIAGRAM III
    Orphans' Wake
Pontoon Anthology 4
    Standing Patterns

Additional Notes

"Finding Beauty, or a Science of Movement," was selected by Mark Doty as an honorable mention for the Tor House Poetry Prize, appearing in the Robinson Jeffers Tor House Foundation newsletter.

"Naming the Everglades" was printed as a limited-edition broadside for Everglades National Park and Artists in Residence in Everglades, Inc. (AIRIE). Designed by Jim Cokas and printed by *lone goose press*.

"Winter in Denali" was printed as a limited-edition broadside for Denali National Park, designed by Jim Cokas and printed by *lone goose press*.

Some of these poems first appeared in the chapbooks: *Halflives* by New Michigan Press and *Flow Variations* by Finishing Line Press.

ABOUT THE AUTHOR

Andrew C. Gottlieb was born in Ontario, Canada, grew up in Massachusetts, and has lived on the western coast of the United States since 1998. He studied writing, and taught composition and creative writing, at both Iowa State University and the University of Washington. Along with the H.J. Andrews Experimental Forest, he's been writer-in-residence in a number of wilderness locations, including three national parks: Denali, Everglades, and Isle Royale. He's also the author of the chapbooks *Flow Variations* (Finishing Line Press) and *Halflives* (New Michigan Press). Say hello at: www.andrewcgottlieb.com.

ABOUT THE PRESS

Trail to Table Press is an imprint of Wandering Aengus Press. We seek to publish literary works that transform our thinking about how we engage with the earth and each other as thoughtful, generous stewards in our actions and interactions, whether on the trail, as consumers and makers, or around the table through genuine connection and respect for life. We wish to share lyric and narrative works that serve both to entertain and enrich others' lives through insight, compassion, and a pure and beautiful expression of experience.

www.ingramcontent.com/pod-product-compliance
Lightning Source LLC
Chambersburg PA
CBHW072018290426
44109CB00018B/2275